J 629.892 MAN
Manatt, Kathleen G.
Robot scientist

102808

21ˢᵗ
Century
Skills Library

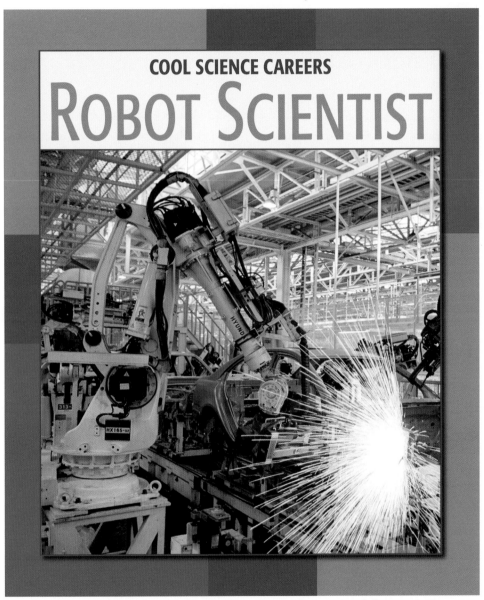

COOL SCIENCE CAREERS

ROBOT SCIENTIST

Kathleen Manatt

Cherry Lake Publishing
Ann Arbor, Michigan

CHERRY
LAKE
Publishing

Published in the United States of America by Cherry Lake Publishing
Ann Arbor, MI
www.cherrylakepublishing.com

Photo Credits: Cover, © Gideon Mendel/Corbis; Title Page, © Gideon Mendel/Corbis;
Page 4,© John Springer Collection/CORBIS; Page 6, © Bettmann/CORBIS; Page 10,
© Tami Chappell/CORBIS; Page 12, © Wyman Ira/CORBIS Sygma; Page 14, © British
Ministry of Defence/Jonathan Holloway/Reuters/CORBIS; Page 16, © Dung Vo Trung/
CORBIS Sygma; Page 18, © Steffen Kugler/epa/CORBIS; Page 20, © Ed Kashi/CORBIS;
Page 24, Photo Courtesy of National Aeronautics and Space Administration (NASA);
Page 26, Photo Courtesy of National Aeronautics and Space Administration (NASA);
Page 28, Photo Courtesy of National Aeronautics and Space Administration (NASA)

Library of Congress Cataloging-in-Publication Data
Manatt, Kathleen G.
  Robot scientist/by Kathleen Manatt.
    p. cm.—(Cool science careers)
  ISBN-13: 978-1-60279-051-3 (hardcover)   978-1-60279-083-4 (pbk.)
  ISBN-10: 1-60279-051-5 (hardcover)   1-60279-083-3 (pbk.)
  1. Robotics—Vocational guidance—Juvenile literature. 2. Mechanical
engineers—Juvenile literature. I. Title. II. Series.
  TJ211.25.M36 2007
  629.8'92—dc22   2007006460

Cherry Lake Publishing would like to acknowledge the work of
The Partnership for 21st Century Skills.
Please visit www.21stcenturyskills.org *for more information.*

TABLE OF CONTENTS

CHAPTER ONE

FAKE AND REAL

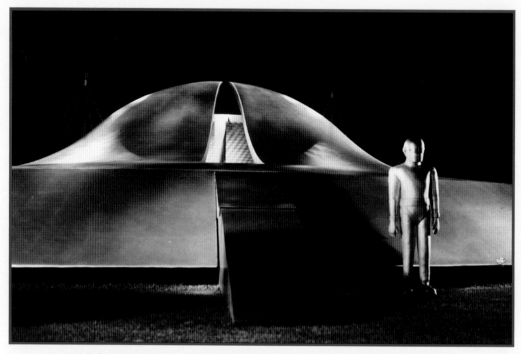

In "The Day the Earth Stood Still," an alien brings a dangerous robot to Earth and promises to use it against us if we don't live in peace.

The **robots** you see in movies and on TV are smart, fantastic, and sometimes dangerous. They may even have personalities. In the "Star Wars" movies, C-3PO is loyal, a worrywort, and seems to talk all the time.

Other movie robots, such as "the Terminator," may try to kill you.

However, those robots are not much like reality. Real robots are not walking, talking, intelligent machines. Mostly, they do hard work and go dangerous places so people won't have to.

Robots have the potential to change our lives. Every year, we find more ways to make robots work for us. They may change the way we work. They are even being used inside our bodies. As **technology** progresses, we find more and more ways to use robots. One thing is for certain: robots are here to stay!

Lots of movie and TV robots are shaped like people. They have a head, two arms, two legs, and a body. Why do you think these robots are often shaped like this? Hint: Think about a person having to operate them.

CHAPTER TWO

ROBOTS GO WAY BACK

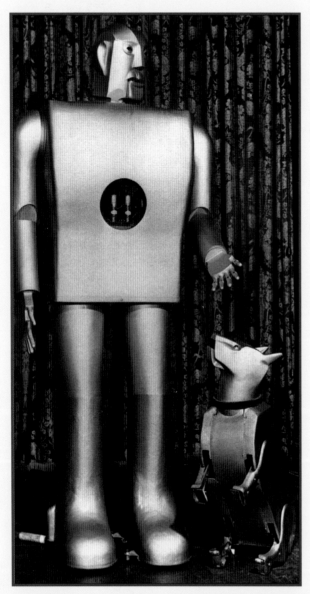

Electro the robot man appeared at the 1939 World's Fair in New York. In 1940, Sparko the dog joined him. Sparko could sit, speak, and beg.

Robots go back a long way. About 400 B.C. a Greek mathematician named Archytas made a mechanical bird powered by steam. He called it The Pigeon.

Leonardo da Vinci also created robots. In about 1495, he drew plans for a **humanoid** robot. Leonardo's robot was to look like a knight in armor. The drawings show how it would sit up, move its arms and legs, and turn its head.

Frenchman Jacques Vaucanson built robots in the 1700s. One was called "The Flute Player." This life-size mechanical man was based on a famous marble statue of the time, but it was really made of wood that was painted white to look like marble. The robot could play a dozen songs. Vaucanson put his robot on display in Paris, and it was a great success and earned a lot of money for its creator.

Life & Career Skills

Vaucanson was a trailblazer in his time. He turned his revolutionary ideas into real, paying business opportunities for himself. Bill Gates became a trailblazer in recent times with his software company. What skills do trailblazers need? Hint: Think about perseverance and creativity.

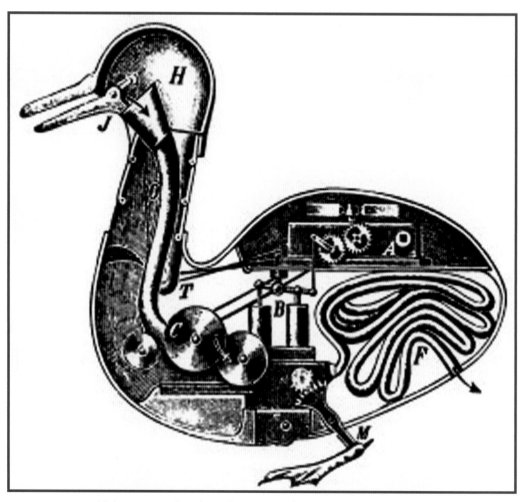

*This cutaway drawing of Vaucanson's Digesting Duck clearly
shows its "throat" and other "internal organs."*

However, Vaucanson's most famous robot was "The Digesting Duck."

This robot was the same size as a real animal. The robot drank water and

quacked. It could flap its wings, which were each made of more than 400 parts. It could stretch out its neck and take grain from your hand. Then the robot duck swallowed the grain, digested it, and pooped!

Vaucanson showed off "The Digesting Duck" in 1739, and people were fascinated. Even France's King Louis XV was an admirer. The king asked Vaucanson to create robots to improve France's silk-making business. Vaucanson did improve the making of silk, but he made silkworkers very angry in the process. They said that no machine could replace them, and they threw rocks at him. He got even by making a silk-making robot that was powered by a donkey.

Learning & Innovation Skills

Silk making was very important to the French economy in the 1700s. Yet Vaucanson used a donkey to power his silk-making robot. What does this say about Vaucanson's feelings towards French silk workers?

CHAPTER THREE

ROBOT CREATORS TODAY

*Today, kids who are interested in robots can buy kits
and build the robots themselves.*

The robot creators of earlier times were mostly self-taught. They experimented and tried different processes until things worked the way they wanted them to.

It's different today. There are even summer camps for young robot creators. Children as young as nine years old can attend. One camp tells young campers to bring their own needle nose pliers, two kinds of screwdrivers, and a tool box to keep them in.

People who want to become robot creators take lots of math and science courses in high school. Then they get college degrees, often in mechanical and electrical engineering and in math. Many also

Some good places to study to be a robot creator in the United States are the Massachusetts Institute of Technology, Carneige Mellon University, and Iowa State Univeristy. There are similar schools in Japan, Finland, Australia, France, and England. To find out more, go to *http://www. cs.cmu.edu/ ~chuck/robotpg/ robofaq/6.html*

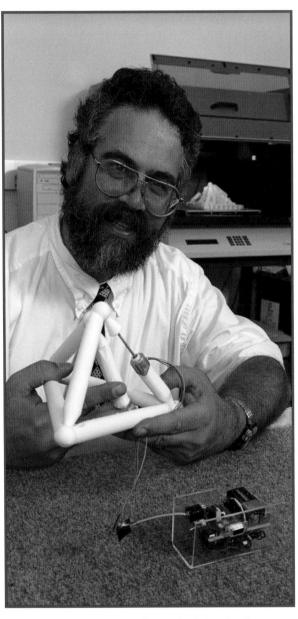

Robot scientist Jordan Pollack is a leader in the field of how to design robots more quickly and at less cost.

get an advanced degree called a Ph.D. During college and graduate school, they often work in univeristy robot labs as part of a team of robot creators. Then they get jobs in one of three places: a university or college, a business, or a government lab.

No matter where they work, grown up robot creators first must decide what kind of robot they are going to create. Will it be just for fun, or will it be used to explore the stars? Maybe the robot will be used in hospitals or in factories. A robot just for fun could be made in bright colors and do silly things, while a robot used in hospitals would need to be very safe and easy to clean.

Then the robot creators will talk to all the people who will use the robot. They will find out what kinds of things the robot needs to do. They will learn about where it will work. They will discuss how big it can be and how much the users can afford to pay. For example, a toy robot needs to be inexpensive and easy to use. A robot we send into outer space needs to work without oxygen and be *very* reliable.

Learning & Innovation Skills

The fictional robots have inspired scientists to create real robots that are productive, helpful, and entertaining. If you owned a business, why might you want to use robots for some tasks? What is the downside of using them?

Some robots, such as this one owned by the British Royal Navy, can be used for underwater rescues.

The the robot creators start drawing plans, which may go through several versions. Eventually, the drawn plans will be turned into a prototype. This gives the robot creators a chance to see how their ideas work in real life. In fact, there may be several prototypes.

Then the real robot is produced. However, the robot creator's job is not done. The robot must be installed and checked. Even after this, the robot creator may be called back to do a "tune up" or solve a problem.

21st Century Content

Some people build robots as a hobby. There are hobby clubs in Dallas, Atlanta, Minneapolis, Phoenix, San Francisco, and many other cities. U.S. clubs meet with clubs from around the world for robot workshops and competitions. Upcoming competitions are scheduled for South Africa, Denmark, Austria as well as Atlanta and Hartford.

CHAPTER FOUR

ROBOTS FOR OUR HEALTH

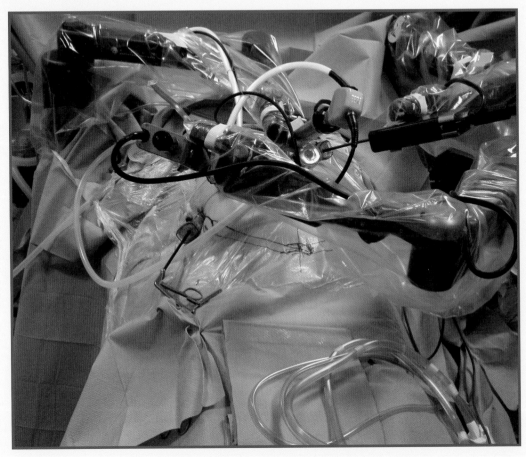

Using a surgical robot, this operation took place in France but the surgeon was in the United States.

Medical robots are big business! Many companies now make medical

robots and sell them around the world. These robots are widely used in surgery and in medical testing. They make surgery safer and less painful. They also make it possible to look for problems inside the body that it would be impossible to find otherwise.

Doctors use thin medical robots in some types of surgery. Then doctors can work inside a human body, but only make a very small cut in the skin. These robots can go inside veins and arteries, even a heart.

The doctor may sit several feet away from the patient and look at a TV that shows things 10 times larger than real. The robot's "eyes" give the doctor a much clearer picture than actually looking inside would.

World-renowned scientist Stephen Hawking has been extremely disabled for decades but his robotic wheelchair allows him to "speak" by moving his face slightly.

How would you like it if your doctor told you to swallow a robot?

That day may be coming soon! The robot will look for problems in your

stomach and intestines. It will have a camera, tiny legs, and tiny feet.

After you swallow the robot, your doctor will use radio signals to move it backwards and forwards to search for problems.

When the doctor has finished, the tiny robot will just

pass out of your system like food waste does.

Medical robots are also used in surgery on hips

and knees. The robots can make necessary cuts on

bones much more precisely than humans can. These

very precise cuts can make the results of the surgery

much more successful. Of course, both patients and

doctors like that very much.

Hospitals in Michigan and California now

have robot doctors. These robots don't replace real

doctors, but they do make it much easier for doctors

and hospital patients to communicate. The robots

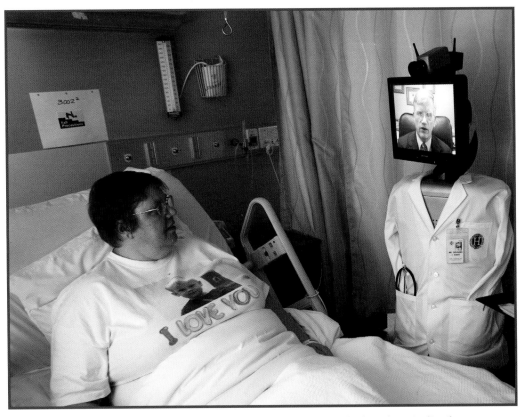

In 2005, some doctors began routinely meeting with their hospitalized patients by robot, as shown here in Hackensack, New Jersey.

weigh about 200 pounds (90.9 kg) and can move at a top speed of

2 miles (3.2 km) per hour. They allow doctors to see patients even

when the doctors are away from the hospitals. All that is needed is

a connection

CHAPTER FIVE

ROBOTS IN BUSINESS

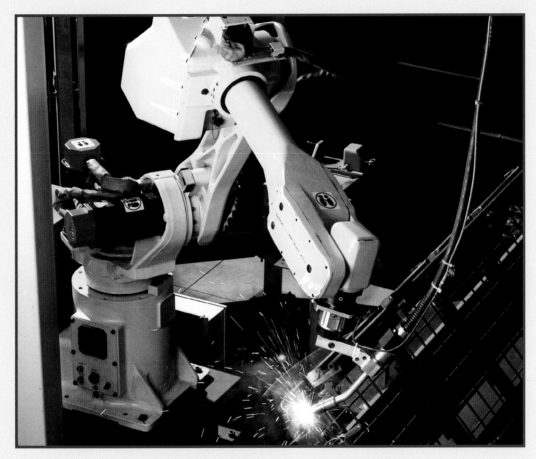

*Robots can be used in manufacturing to do jobs that
are dangerous or would be boring to people.*

Robots have been used in **manufacturing** for decades. In fact, the first

industrial robot was used in a General Motors (GM) factory in 1961.

Today, GM uses thousands of robots in the process of building cars and trucks. They weld pieces of metal together. They can reach inside spaces where people are too big to fit. They operate in paint booths, saving humans from nasty paint fumes.

In England, one company makes about 40 million sandwiches a year for later sales by a grocery store chain. In 2001, the company began making the sandwiches with robots. People liked the result. The robots made the sandwiches faster, so they were fresher when they got to customers. Plus, fewer people handled the sandwiches, so there was less danger of passing on germs.

Would you like a robot to clean your house? Well, one is already available. It's called Roomba®, and it took about a dozen years to create. Three scientists from the Massachusetts Institute of Technology went into business together to develop it. This device has been on the market since 2002. It scoots around on the floor, vacuuming as it goes. When it thinks the floor is clean, it shuts itself off.

The iRobot Roomba® vacuums up dirt, pet hair, and other debris and is advertised as knowing where to vacuum and where not.

CHAPTER SIX

WAY OUT ROBOTS

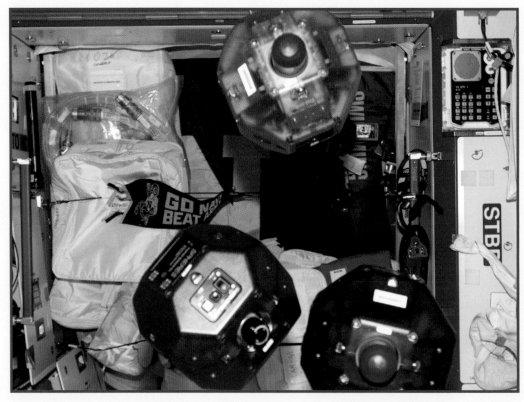

NASA created the softball-sized Personal Satellite Assistant to monitor air pressure and temperature, etc. for astronauts.

When it comes to space exploration, robots are just fine. They can travel for months or even years in space without food or oxygen. They never miss their friends and family, and they never get bored. Why might boredom be a problem on space flights? Think

about being cooped up in your bedroom for several

months. That's what space flight might be like.

The U.S. Space Shuttle has one very big robot. It's

called the Remote Manipulator System, or RMS. It

helps to move big things out of the shuttle and into

the International Space Station. It can also hold an

astronaut in place when he or she works in space.

The RMS can reach out as far as 45 feet (13.7 meters),

but it is operated by a crew member from inside the

Space Shuttle.

The United States has also landed several robots

on the planet Mars. These robots are called **landers,**

Computers guide robots, including the space shuttles. However, scientists watch the shuttle's progress every second, ready to make adjustments as needed. What is the most important skill these scientists have?

The RMS folds into the shuttle for take off and landing.
It has been used on more than 50 space missions.

21st CENTURY SKILLS LIBRARY

and they have traveled over the planet's surface to investigate what is there. The landers must get instructions from their human managers on Earth, and the instructions take many minutes to travel to Mars. Sometimes, the human managers got quite nervous while waiting for **verification** that the instructions had been received.

The Mars landers rolled across the Martian landscape, and they performed several tests. They took thousands of pictures and sent them back to Earth. They swept up dust and analyzed it. They dug little holes in rocks to get more material to analyze. They also searched for water. Finding water—even a

Two of the Mars landers are named Spirit and Opportunity. Why do you think the scientists gave the landers these names? To find out more about the Mars projects and to play some cool games, go to *http:// marsprogram.jpl. nasa.gov/funzone_ flash.html*

The Mars robots had to travel about 33.9 million miles (54.5 million km) before they could begin their work.

tiny, tiny bit—is very important because it could help scientists determine if some sort of life once lived on the "Red Planet."

All of the lander tasks had been planned years ahead of time by their robot creators. The scientists practiced the tasks many times with landers here on Earth. Then the real landers were packed up and sent off into space.

Many months later, the robot creators got to try out their inventions and look for answers to important scientific questions. Sometimes, the answers only brought up more questions. Now the robot creators are designing new Mars landers that will help answer those.

Life & Career Skills

The men and women who work on the robots that go to Mars see their jobs as the culmination of a lifelong dream. These robot creators have spent many years in school. When they looked for work, they had to compete with many, many others who wanted the same jobs. What kinds of life skills do the successful robot creators probably have that helped them reach their goals?

Glossary

humanoid (HYOO-muh-noid) having human characteristics or form

landers (LAN-derz) name give to robots that the U.S. has sent to the planet Mars

manufacturing (man-yuh-FAK-cher-eng) making or processing raw materials into a finished product, especially by means of a large-scale industrial operation

prototype (PROH-tuh-tahyp) original form that serves as the basis for later stages

robots (ROH-bots) machines that operate automatically or by remote control

technology (tek-NOL-uh-jee) the application of science, especially to industrial or commercial objectives

verification (ver-uh-fi-KEY-shuhn) confirmation of an act; to support or establish the truth of

Other Resources

Books

Domaine, Helena. *Robotics.*
Minneapolis, MN: Learner Publications, 2006.

Eckold, Dan. *Ultimate Robot Kit.* New York: Dorling Kindersley, 2001.

Gifford, Clive. *How to Build a Robot.*
New York: Franklin Watts, 2001.

Jones, David. *Mighty Robots: Mechanical Marvels that
Fascinate and Frighten.* Toronto: Annick Press, 2005.

Oliver, Mark. *Robot Dog.* Intercourse, PA: Good Books, 2005.

Pilkey, Dav. *Ricky Ricotta's Mighty Robot Vs. Stupid Stinkbug
From Saturn #6.* New York: Scholastic, 2001.

Simon, Seymour. *Destination: Mars.* New York: Harper Collins, 2000.

Other Media

The Day the Earth Stood Still, starring Michael Rennie
and Patricia Neal. 20th Century Fox, 1951.

Forbidden Planet, starring Walter Pigeon and Anne Francis.
Metro-Goldwyn-Mayer, 1956.

http://www.botball.org/ is a website about
NASA-sponsored robot-building contests for students.

http://www.mos.org/sln/Leonardo/LeoHomePage.html is a website
about Leonardo da Vinci from Boston's Museum of Science.

INDEX

ABOUT THE AUTHOR

Kathleen Manatt is a long-time writer, editor, and publisher of books for children. Many of her books have been about faraway places, which she likes to visit. She grew up in Illinois, Iowa, New Jersey, and California, and lived in Chicago for many years as an adult. She has climbed pyramids in Mexico, ridden elephants in Thailand, and toured the fjords of Norway. She has also visited Moscow, Lisbon, Paris, Geneva, London, Madrid, Edinburgh, and Barcelona. She now lives in Austin, Texas.